AND THEN I FELL

MONOLOGUES

for

GROWN-UPS

Volume 1

SYLVIA VALEVICIUS

DEDICATION

~To the Indie Authors around the Globe whose

Creativity Rocks our World~

AUTHOR'S NOTE

The monologues in this volume are works of fiction. The characters, herein, are creations of imagination. Their experiences, however, reflect the internal and external struggles of what it means to be human. In that sense you, Reader, may discover someone you know, even yourself.

As you expect, a monologue is the voice of *one* speaker. Unlike the soliloquy which reflects the thoughts of a speaker, *alone,* a monologue implies there is an audience present, a silent *listener.* These monologues name a context wherein the speaker shares a story, and hopes for a reaction from the listener, be it comfort, sorrow, outrage, shock, or just understanding of the speaker's plight.

Often monologues are performing arts pieces, and useful for auditions. My *Monologues for Youth* Volumes 1 & 2 appear in that format. Easy to memorize, the teenage monologues contain a sense of immediacy where a young speaker expresses a matter of some urgency.

These *Monologues for Grown-Ups*, Vol. 1 differ slightly as they are more reflective, adult-themed, and several lend themselves to the short-story genre. Of course, they can be adapted for workshops, auditions, performances, group-reading for your book club, or perhaps even for 'open mic' night.

Finally, the monologues are useful as springboards for discussion on life – as a grown-up.

> *'It takes courage to grow up and become who you really are.'*
>
> ~ee cummings

ACKNOWLEDGMENTS

Thanks to my family who felt my absence during those intense creative moments and kindly tolerated my disappearance during the crunch.

Thanks to the 'Oakville Writers and Poets Group' for their reader-suggestions and warm encouragement.

Thanks to supportive friends who get excited about my writing – too many to name, but they know they are great!

And thanks to Erma, writer/author/translator, who generously read my manuscript with her astute eye for editing. However, as the author of this work, any last-minute changes or possible typos are solely my responsibility.

SYLVIA VALEVICIUS

CONTENTS

THE GIFTS of SUMMER SCHOOL

~female, late 40s gives lunch talk to retired elementary teachers~

Time: The Present

Ah, Summer School. It is intense. Five weeks, five hours each day, five days a week. All with the same teacher and class. Both teachers and students either love it or resent it. I wanted to teach kids who loved it. Wouldn't you? Rarely a discipline problem with lates, absences, or incomplete assignments.

With its stricter rules, Summer School holds less distraction, affords more in-depth discussion, encourages group work, and offers opportunity to develop ideas; furthermore, assignment-completion happens right on the spot! For me, those were the finest times in my teaching career.

As an academic English teacher in the secondary panel, I applied outside my homeschool, and requested 'new credit' courses, not the do-overs. To avoid burn-out from the regular school season, for the summer classes, I needed the gift of students who were academically motivated. There are specialized teachers with more patience than I to assist students in repeat courses. Most students were eager to succeed during these five weeks. The less committed eliminated themselves by end of week one.

Still, as the saying goes, 'you meet the nicest people' in contexts you wouldn't expect. One July, in a small university town, I recall my Summer School senior English class as filled with both joy, and great sorrow. Along with the wonderful gifts of ambition, energy, and interest I received from the entire class that hot summer, I also was privileged to meet some highly individualistic, exceptional human beings. Let me tell you about three young men who touched my heart. Is there a greater gift than that?

It was a surprise for me to see a student about my age. Gary, slight and bearded, sat at the back, and brought a down-to-earth gentle maturity to the group discussions with the teenagers in class. A quiet man, Gary didn't offer much about his personal self or his background. Yet, one day, he gifted me – (oh, goodie, a teacher gift, I smiled to myself), something rarely seen at the high school level. He handed me a book he purchased and inscribed, on men and their goddesses. It's not what you might think. The book revealed the feminist and feminine aspects in the male. How refreshing. Thus, I came to understand Gary through his gift. It was his way of describing himself, and his depth of thinking, not just a mature student sitting at the back working to complete his high school credits.

Now quite the opposite from Gary, in the front seat, sat Fraser. Eighteen years old, a mountain-sized youth, broad-shouldered with long hair that hung loosely over his dark eyes, and beyond his neck, Fraser was a hard-working charmer of Aboriginal descent. Although determined to be successful, Fraser slipped in late on a couple of Monday mornings. The air in the humid classroom filled with remnants of bonfire and booze. Fraser explained he came straight to class from a weekend pow-wow. He elaborated on the spiritual ceremonial regalia of his culture: visits with friends as they beat drums, sang, and circle-danced together.

To apologize for his lates, Fraser gifted me with one of his stunning works of art as a peace-offering: a magnificent white dove, celestial wings extended, bordered in black. I thrilled at his talent, and treasured this gift. He succeeded to gain his credit as well.

The third boy who remains in my heart from that summer was not from our English class, but from physics next door. He wondered if he might join a field trip I planned to the theatre. The play: *World of Wonders,* a mystical show. Asian, tall, ethereal, Matthew was a delight. Since he was new to the group, we sat together on the bus. A visionary, he spoke of his love of medicine, magic, and the arts. I thought he would have a wonderful future. His gift to me was the sharing of his dreams.

Before summer school ended, Matthew lost his life walking on train tracks with some friends. His death shocked me and the community. I attended his funeral, and was overwhelmed with anguish and humility. His parents, desperate to find some tangible thing or person their child last knew, clung to me, the teacher. I had little to offer but sympathy which seemed so inadequate.

In reflection, dear teachers, that special year reminds me of the three Magi with their gifts: Gary with gold, symbol of kingship on earth; Fraser with frankincense, symbol of deity; and Matthew with myrrh, the embalming oil and symbol of death. These were three special people from Summer School, and the gift I learned from them: the beauty of the human heart.

BLACKOUT

VANITY

~self-absorbed female, 35, chats with new Toronto friend~

Time: Circa 1980s

When I got newly-separated in the mid-Seventies, Liz, I treated myself to lunch at Hess Village. It's this place in Hamilton where cool people *still* go to be seen. Lucky my babysitter, Mrs. Wendall, back from holiday, away *too long,* (stretches this out) gave me back some time to *myself,* finally! (rolls her eyes) I mean I love the kids, and all, but single parenting is tough. We all need a break, right, Lizzie?

So, there I was at *Lloyd's Café,* my nails just done, admiring the pink enamel against the white tablecloth, holding up a delicate tea-cup in my other hand, glancing around the room to see who might notice me, when I spotted a girlfriend from my childhood. Sabrina had changed a lot, so at first, I wasn't even sure it was her. She approached my table with that crazy, impish grin I remember best on a small, eight-year-old in pigtails. Oh, Lizzie, but those cat-like, narrowed hazel eyes were hers, alright! She was so tall now, strong-boned. You know, Liz, me and Sabrina used to prank the neighbours when we lived in our north-end crummy neighbourhood. We'd hop fences, rip through backyard gardens, disregarding the pretty flower beds. Oh, we were a pair of tough little devils! Too bad my parents moved when we were around ten – of course, since they relocated us to an upscale neighbourhood, Sabrina and I lost touch.

When I got up to hug her, Liz, Sabrina squeezed me to bits! I coughed, we both laughed, a bit embarrassed. Then she dug into her purse, pulled out a pen, a book of matches and scribbled down her address. She insisted that I come to her party Saturday night because we had so much catching up to do. Sabrina spoke so fast, Liz, like she'd had too much coffee. Then she looked me up and down, and said she had friends I *must* meet. So, of course, she had me interested. I said sure, I'll do my best. I hoped she had well-heeled people in her life now. Know what I mean, Liz?

Well, Lizzie, I must tell you I was shocked when I climbed out of the cab that Saturday night. Sabrina's home, apparently once a turn-of the-century mansion, was now converted into cheap, rental units. The musty hallway was dark and dingy, but I continued towards some strains of electronic sitar music. It felt eerie, and there was a familiar pungent smell, I almost felt like heaving and leaving…really, don't laugh! I knocked a few times, and figured no one could hear because of the noise inside. But then, Liz, I jumped back because Sabrina suddenly flung open her door, grabbed my arm, and pulled me inside into her psychedelic atmosphere of purple haze and ganja smoke.

Sabrina began to introduce me to her guests who stared right through me, glassy-eyed, with slack-jawed expressions. I must have appeared quite a contrast to barefoot Sabrina in her *flower power* dress which draped to her ankles, and whose loose black hair masked half her face. There I stood in my navy-blue pant suit, looking dressed for church, in comparison.

Anyway, Liz, from this foggy crowd, a stocky older guy came towards me stroking his salt and pepper beard; he sauntered with an out-stretched arm like he was expecting me already. Sabrina introduced him with a bit of flair, know what I mean, Liz? She laid it on that this was her *artist extraordinaire.* This guy kissed my hand and said to call him Fausto. Then he lowered his thick eyebrows, called me a beauty, and said he *must* do an oil painting of me. Honestly, Liz, he had me at *beauty;* with a divorce pending my vanity was in desperate need of repair. I soaked up this attention, and agreed to sit for him the next week.

Now Fausto's apartment had its own creepiness, Liz, but I put it down to a typical 'artist studio.' It was in a deserted area of downtown, in an old office building where I had to mount about three flights of creaky, wooden stairs. Struck me as a bit of a fire trap, know what I mean, Liz? The attic was all exposed pipes, and except for an easel, canvas, and a ratty couch, the room was sparse.

Fausto had me sit on a hard stool for an hour each time I went there. I was supposed to hold a gaze looking forward. Darn agonizing to pose for so long, but you know, Lizzie, my vanity kicked in, so I did as he asked. I just thought how great a gift this would be for me! I was so glad he chose me because I was Sabrina's old friend, *and* because he found me hot! Totally flattering, don't you think? I just couldn't wait to hang the painting in my new place. It really felt exciting, Liz.

The final night of sitting for my portrait Fausto offered me a silver chalice of wine. The silver was tarnished, and the wine tasted odd, a bit tinny, but I didn't care; I was feeling relaxed. I kept sipping away as Fausto continued with his brush strokes. Since he instructed me to look straight ahead, I couldn't smile at my artist or anything; I could only see him out of my peripheral vision.

Then something horrible happened, Liz. Fausto's head just grew. I mean it mushroomed way out of proportion. I thought I was imagining things, and started to sweat. Didn't know whether I should tell him my visions. I thought he'd put me down as a nutcase. But then his ears morphed into those of a mammoth monkey, Liz. I was terrified and turned to face him. What a surprise – he looked normal then, and growled at me to turn back to my profile. I felt really intimidated by his tone, Liz. So, I obeyed the artist, turned back, and took another sip of this wine to calm down.

But his head kept expanding, up to the ceiling. Then I really freaked out, and shrieked, turned to face him. He looked ordinary but totally pissed off. He said we're finished and to come and view the painting. I hobbled over to the canvas, weak with fear, and looked; it was nice, sort of impressionistic, you know? I felt like an idiot. He told me it's mine for a couple of hundred dollars.

That's when I grabbed my purse and ran, Liz. I almost tumbled down the two hundred steps out into the street, and never looked back to Fausto or Sabrina, the scammers. He wanted money! Can you believe it? I may have hallucinated that night, but I realized I wasn't going to pay that pair a cent for drugging me!

Jeez, now when I think back, that portrait would have looked great in my new place. What would you have done if you were me, Lizzie?

BLACKOUT

TRUTH BE TOLD

~male, 40ish, reveals his issues in group therapy~

Time: The Present

Hi. I'm Jimmy. I'm Greek and I work in my dad's restaurant. (pause) It's okay to laugh. I know it's a stereotype. But what isn't is that I'm gay. (pause) No need to look so serious. I'm out and I'm proud! (chuckles at his cliché) I've been out to my parents since I've been sixteen. I know that sounds rare, especially for an immigrant family, but the best part is I KNOW my parents love me.

So why am I here? What happened to me? I survived a terrible accident. But let me go back a few years.

My dad is my hero because he opened his small restaurant, *Souvlaki and Salads,* just at the edge of 'Gay Village.' I know he did this for me, to understand my community. Both gays and straights eat there. And my dad was happy to keep an eye on me. My sister died in a car accident when she was twelve; my parents didn't want to lose their last child.

So, a few years ago, this straight-looking guy with a tidy beard started showing up alone. We got talking. He was about ten years older than me. He liked me, I could tell. He was careful because he was a college professor, still in the closet. Truth be told, he was more worried about his Eastern European mother suspecting.

Jerry became my lover. We actually *fell* in love. He told me he could see a future with us together, either when he retires, and we move to the tropics, or when his mother passes on. I hated watching Jerry play the straight man while his mother looked healthier than ever. Of course, I never *met* her, but he showed me photos on his phone of where he got his handsome looks. I guess he was trying to get me to like her. NOT likely!

But we did go to bars and the fabulous Toronto Gay Pride parade every year; we got lost in the crowds. And it's not like his mom would *ever* watch that parade on TV, either.

So, last summer Jerry bought a boat. Neither one of us knew much about boats, but Jerry said it was a Carver 32Aft Cabin, which was large enough to sleep in, and he kept it at the marina in the next town. It was a beauty. He named it with both our initials. It was called *J J Cinema.* That made me feel like we really belonged together. And cinema because Jerry taught film courses and theatre arts at his community college.

At first, we didn't go out much in the boat. We liked to sit in it and just get used to it. We brought along my cute little pug, Jeepers. We talked a lot. Poor Jerry had to keep explaining himself, and I tried being understanding. Like the time his family doctor, who was a nice enough guy, but was *clueless* that Jerry was gay, kept trying to set him up with some chick. The doctor was trying to do a favour for his wife's niece – find her a nice guy, right? Jerry finally caved, and contacted her. I was none too pleased.

In fact, I was so pissed off the day she showed up at the SLIP. (pause) Oh, that's where you dock the boat. He invited her for a drink. She was cute, I guess, if you're straight. Sort of sassy. Hard to imagine she couldn't find her own guy. Anyway, she brought him some foreign film – a DVD- they had texted about. Then, I came walking down the dock with Jeepers, and she took one look at me, and then at Jerry, and damn it, she knew instantly! Her raised eyebrow said it all!

I gave her daggers when she looked at me again. Then I brushed past her and took Jeepers onto the boat. Ever the gentleman, Jerry invited her to come back later, but she turned on her heel and said no thanks, and keep the movie boys. She didn't even pet Jeepers. I was relieved when she took off in a huff, swinging her little ass.

Well, Jerry was shook up. What was he going to tell his doctor? Would this incident blow his cover? With his nerves all frayed, Jerry said let's just get this boat out, and have ourselves a good time! He turned on the first engine, and Jeepers got excited and barked. When he turned on the second engine, the propane tank exploded. We were all blown into the water. I was told later the smoke from the propane was blinding.

I don't remember anymore, only what others tell me, and what I read on the internet. The ORNGE medical helicopter flew me to Emerge. I had multiple burns on my legs and many broken bones. I know my heart is a muscle, but it broke too.

Of course, I didn't make it to Jerry's funeral. I miss him and Jeepers. They both drowned. After months in hospital, I was suicidal and was transferred to the psych-ward. So here I am, folks, trying to deal with this shit.

Truth be told, none of this would have happened if Jerry would've been *out* to his mother, in the first place. She wrecked my life…the Bitch. Sorry guys…I think I need to hear somebody else's problem to get over my own. Who's next?

BLACKOUT

THE AFFAIR

~adult female shares her past adventures in coffee &
conversation group~

Time: The Present with Reflections on the Seventies

"DIVORCED! My mommy's divorced!"

Such was the newsflash my six-year old unstoppable
son Lucas let slip to the new friends we made while travelling.

I was sharing some drinks and conversation with a
lovely husband and wife, both lawyers, we met in the Munich
Beer Gardens. Not much of a beer-guzzler, I soon needed to
visit the rest-room, and Lucas was playing a runabout game
with the Kellers' five-year-old daughter, Stephanie, so they
told me - just go ahead, we'll watch the kids.

When I returned to the picnic table, that's when the
Kellers laughed and told me about Lucas's enthusiastic
declarations. They were excited to learn this information, and

now insisted that I meet a friend of theirs visiting from out of town. Okay… I was open to meeting new people. After all, I was supposed to be on an adventure…of sorts.

After my divorce, and with a small inheritance from a deceased dear cousin, I decided I would take my young son with me for a month to Europe. I was a mature university student now, and summertime was an opportunity to explore some roots in Germany. We flew to Frankfurt, I rented a car and drove south through the Black Forest, making little overnight stops along the way at charming Bavarian 'Bed & Breakfast' inns. But by the time we got to Munich, tired from driving, I wanted a little pampering, so I pulled out my credit card, and booked us a luxury room at the Munich Hilton for a few days. Lucas loved the bubble baths in our hotel room. He said much better Mommy than the 'everybody's toilets down the hall' in those guest-houses. And, we had our own beds at the Hilton. Although, during most of the trip, we never minded snuggling-up in one bed under an oversized duvet.

The Kellers said that their friend was from Kuwait, and they suggested they would send a reliable girl to my hotel room to sit with Lucas while the four of us went to dinner in the hotel's fine dining-room. Frankly, in those days, I had no idea where Kuwait existed geographically, but I smiled and faked it until I returned to the hotel and checked with the concierge. A small, wealthy middle-eastern country. And this friend of the Kellers, who they said was called Khalid Haddad, was an Arab. How exotic this all sounded to me! I thought he would probably have brown skin. Arabs only appeared in story-books when I was growing up. In my white Ontario town, I never even saw a Black person, never mind an Arab. The only people with a shade of skin barely darker than my own were folks from our sizable Italian community.

Khalid was not particularly good-looking, a bit thin and short for my tastes, but he was charismatic, all smiles and sizzling. We soon found ourselves alone after dinner when the Kellers decided to disappear and allow us to get to know each other. Fortunately, Khalid was registered at the Hilton too, so I was comfortable with continuing our visit in his room. He opened a bottle of expensive champagne from the mini-bar for which I really didn't give a hoot. I guess he expected me to be all lah-dee-dah about it. I could see his face drop in disappointment when I didn't gush.

He told me about himself. He said he was still single, a colonel in the Kuwaiti Air Force. That was impressive. He also said how he loved his nieces and nephews; I guess he made a point of it because I had a son close by, hoping it would look good on him. It did. I felt his sincere kindness.

He described his travels to Thailand, and his experiences with people who seemed double-gendered. 'Shemale', I believe he called them. I didn't mind having casual sex with Khalid, but I'm glad he told me those stories afterwards. It did cross my mind the potential dangers of indiscriminate sex - this in the late seventies just before the AIDS acronym burst on the scene as a household term for a deadly illness related to sexual activity. Man!

What really did bother me most was that I was cheating. I dislike that term, find it disgusting. I was divorced alright, but not totally free; I had left a sweet boyfriend of eight months behind. Lucas and I stayed in Munich a few extra days to hang out with Khalid. I had to telegram my boyfriend not to pick us up at the airport at the arranged date. It was a mess when I got home. I used the cheap excuse that I loved the country so much. I felt like a mean rat.

Some months later, Khalid was flying to North America and wanted me to join him in Washington, D.C. He sent me flight tickets. I had to make some bullshit excuse to my boyfriend and off I flew for a long weekend. Khalid, now with his entourage, and I, stayed in the infamous Watergate Hotel. I expected it to be something grand, but it was a boutique hotel, quiet, not what one expected from the dramatic, political news reports of the day.

Khalid took me shopping, told me to buy whatever I wanted. I bought toys for Lucas. Khalid wanted me to choose something of jewellery, perfume for myself, but I did not want to feel bought. I even passed up his offer to fly with him on the Concord to London. If anyone remembers that aircraft, no longer available, where you could cross the Atlantic in half the time.

Overall, I guess I made a poor job of being a rich man's mistress. But I did a worse job of being a nice guy's girlfriend. Eventually, we broke up. Cheating didn't sit well with me. Although, I realized my behaviour was symbolic, significant. I understood it didn't matter what any man had to offer, I didn't want to belong to anyone but myself.

I wanted more of life's experiences. I wanted to see more of the world.

And I did.

BLACKOUT

SYLVIA VALEVICIUS

SHRINK CITY

~female, 50s, panelist on Mental Health Experiences
Conference~

Time: The Present – Reflection over Decades.

I'm pleased to be on this panel. Over the years, I've had quite a lot of interaction with mental health professionals, and I have to say, it has not always been a pretty picture, or easy, getting help for my mental issues. It feels good, and timely, to examine how this procedure can be improved.

Most of the need I had for professional help occurred when I was in my twenties and thirties. I was unsure of myself, and I suffered from anxiety and depression which began in my teens, then increased when I was a young wife, and new mother. And later, after my divorce, I felt my world had collapsed. I had several nervous break-downs over the decades ahead, but rarely did I feel comfortable with the so-called support I received. I was a highly-sensitive personality on the inside, but did not appear so to others. I was so eager to please to gain acceptance of my true self.

Back when I had two babies and my husband was still in school, he decided to move us from our small but neat apartment into his mother's unruly household. Overrun by three unkempt cats, and a large dog, my mother-in-law's place was filled with chaos and confusion. The atmosphere was unhealthy for the kids: I'm talking garbage, pizza boxes stacked and smelly, unwashed dishes, animal food cans left open. I struggled to keep a clean environment for all of us. My mother-in-law and the son she doted on banded together against me. They took offense at my efforts to keep a clean home. I was disrespected and mocked for trying to make changes. One night I just lost it, pulled a butcher knife from the kitchen drawer, and went for the two of them. My breakdown is a whole other story. Not only did they want me to see a psychiatrist, I begged for help, myself. I felt overwhelmed, reduced to nothing. There was an insurmountable sense of fear in my head.

Dr. Angus seemed nice. I soon realized that was only his outward appearance, since he had slicked-down hair, and dressed primly in a jacket and tie. He asked me to describe how I would like to be. Clearly nervous, and not understanding, I answered I had dreams of being an actor or a singer. Suddenly, it felt like a 'game show', because that wasn't the right answer. Not at all! He smirked and barked about *qualities* I should aim for like tolerance *-you're stupid was implied.* His sneer then took on a male dominance. Don't wear a skirt in here anymore, he ordered. I don't want to be distracted by your legs. I can't do my job, he scolded. *My fault for dressing lady-like to see the doctor as my proper mother had taught me?*

Next, I sought out a therapist from the university's mental-help centre, and entered a doctor-patient relationship for three years. The psychiatrist appointed me was a quiet, bearded man with bushy hair who smoked a pipe and stared at me. He asked few questions. Eventually, I thought this must be the therapy: let the patient babble on. So, I was forced to talk to myself, and watch him stuff his pipe, between puffs. Somewhere close to the end of this period, he spoke.

He was surprised, after all this time, I had not 'transferred' my feelings onto him, had not fallen in love with him. He wasn't the only one surprised. I never dreamed that was an expectation!

And even if it were the case, back then, with my having some narrow attitudes, his ethnicity was not on my radar as crush-material. As a people-pleaser, a condition I believe got me to this anxiety state to begin with, I felt bad, and ashamed. I disappointed him. I began to think how, historically, his people were persecuted. Now, I was crushed thinking I hurt his feelings. I needed a solution.

Late one Saturday evening, I called the doctor's service. They took my number and said he'd return my call, which he did. I went into my act, told him the biggest lie of my life. I said I realized I was in love with him, and waited for his response. He rose to the occasion; he gave his best patronizing reply with a righteous tone – perfect. Nothing could possibly come of this he informed me. He and his wife were happily married. End of story.

What a relief! To have that issue done with, I could relax before my last session with this shrink. His parting words of 'wisdom,' as it were, failed to impress me when he announced: 'When you first came here, I wouldn't have given a penny for your thoughts, but now…'

He continued to some lame praise; I drowned him out relieved to escape him, and his stuffy, smoke-filled room. He could keep his compliments to himself. And his wife, for that matter.

Years later, when I had to leave work for mental stress, there were group therapy sessions hosted by another hospital. These were mandated, or I would not have received insurance compensation during my period of illness and unemployment.

In one such session, a patient turned to me with disdain, followed by all pairs of eyes in the circle, to announce: 'You're not that great!' So baffling and provoking came this smack of a snowball statement, that I swivelled in my chair, my back to everyone, and felt them pity me as my shoulders shook while I wept in pain. My thoughts were: did I even *say* I was? On what grounds was this crowd judging me? And what right did they have? Due to that cruelty, I swore off group therapy.

Well, that didn't last! Because another work-induced stress situation arose where I tried a different group where the sessions were touted as a real health benefit. Can't say I didn't try! Here, like the previous place, a woman participant verbally attacked me, unleashed her anger and hurled this insult: 'You'll never amount to anything!' she yelled at me.

I was stunned by her ignorance, not to mention her viciousness. For in the grand scheme of life, by now, I had accomplished a great deal in terms of education and career goals. But she had no knowledge of these facts as she spat her abuse. Feeling sensitive and vulnerable at the time, I was terribly hurt. It's only in retrospect that I realize those comments had *nothing* to do with me, at all, and she was probably spewing out words that had been abusively dumped on her in the past, poor woman.

But back then, I turned to the moderator of our group, for support, an older gentleman, a social worker on staff. His chin drooped onto his chest, his eyes were closed, his breathing barely audible. Hah! Lucky for him, during the heated session of our group which he was *supervising*, he managed to squeeze in that two o'clock afternoon nap that we all so desperately needed!

So, as you can see from some of my incidents with therapy, getting proper help hasn't always been exactly a picnic. It's good we're talking about changes. I'm pleased with this dialogue. Thank you for listening.

BLACKOUT

DAFFODILS

~upscale mature female speaks at her Bridge Club~

Time: The Present- Reflection on the Sixties

So, my turn to speak, and suddenly this outspoken woman feels shy…alright ladies, I'll share an incident from my early life that stayed with me all these years. New members, please hold your judgment till the end. Thank you.

At twenty-three, I lived in Toronto with my dashing husband, a sensation as a top realtor. He died of a sudden heart-attack fifteen years ago…We lived in a splendid Tudor-style house in the beautiful, leafy area of downtown. I had household help twice a week because I was expecting our third child. Our two little girls, Chrissy and Sissy, took their fair colouring from their dad's Scandinavian ancestry. Believe it or not, *this* white hair was jet-black in those days, long and straight with a fringe to my eyebrows. We used to call a fringe, bangs, then. It was very 60s, very *Cher*. I noticed stares when I went shopping. I guess I was a dead-ringer for that celebrated singer, especially with the heavy black eye-liner we used to wear then.

To reach his level of success, my man worked a lot. Occasionally, he arranged a dinner-date with some important client. He wanted my presence to boost his image. I'd get my lady to watch the girls, and join him. I was flattered that he felt a need for me at his side to score a business deal.

One evening, well into the pregnancy and feeling heavy, I was slow in dressing, but I managed to slide my silk, black and white geometric shift over my expanding tummy, and twisted my hair into an elegant chignon. Off we went to one of those fancy hotels which don't even exist today. I met Brian and his girlfriend, Katy. I'm not claiming to be particularly psychic, but when I met this pair, I had a strong sense that something seemed off.

Katy glowed beside me in the ladies' room. With her translucent skin and fire-orange wild hair, she appeared like Botticelli's iconic, *Venus*. I didn't think much of it then, other than she was dating the wrong person.

Well, I often think of her now. She emerged as a sensual soul who reached out to me. I remember her long fingers as she circled my wrist, and with a gentle tug urged me to turn, meet her green eyes, search for a stray lash. Her gaze held me, my pulse skipped and sparked a flame in my belly. I dismissed these butterflies, the significance of the moment, full of myself, and my unborn child.

Katy came to call on me when Brian and my Rasmus drove out of town specking a land deal. She appeared at my door. She wanted to comfort me she said, help me through the rest of this pregnancy. With the girls in daycare, we were alone. Katy wanted to talk. She said she was not in love with Brian. She was, instead, attracted to me. She appeared tortured, emotionally naked, yet somehow her lips glistened with defiance.

What was that supposed to mean? I dismissed her feelings as nonsense. Not to her face, but to myself, and changed the subject. Offered her a cup of strong tea. When she left, her vanilla-lavender scent remained, which to this day, excites me.

How is it we frequently lose the moment, and don't fully appreciate what's happening? The moment passes and only in reflection we understand. Perhaps that's what Wordsworth meant in his *Daffodils* poem:

'I wandered lonely as a cloud

That floats on high o'er vales and hills

When all at once I saw a crowd

A host of golden daffodils…'

Katy used every opportunity to display the intensity
of her feelings for me. She learned Rasmus would be in
Europe for two weeks; she came to my home again.

More Wordsworth, and note his quaint, *original*
meaning of a word we've adopted for same-sex attraction:

'A poet could not be but gay

In such jocund company

I gazed – and gazed - but little thought

What wealth the show to me had brought.'

Katy, her mystic energy, and flaming hair could
shame even the daffodils with her beauty and boldness. I was
upstairs, putting fresh laundry into the drawers. Katy asked to
lie down beside me on my marriage bed, the sheets still warm.
She exuded a longing for me which never was present with
my husband. I shook my head no, my head which was up my
ass back then! How did I miss that opportunity to hold her,
lessen her anguish, and feel her love? I let her go, but never

forgot.

As Wordsworth closes his poem, today I understand the moment I missed. I retain a divine memory of Katy:

'For oft, when on my couch I lie

In vacant or in pensive mood,

They flash upon that inward eye, which is the bliss of solitude,

And then my heart with pleasure fills,

And dances with the daffodils.'

And in my heart, I often gaze upon my beautiful gay friend, and wonder how her life turned out. Time brings us back the daffodils in our mind's eye, and the ones we loved.

This was personal, ladies. My hope for the younger ones here today is not to lose the moment. It's nice to reflect, but if I could go back, I would. I'd want to touch my golden daffodil, and seek luxurious joy in her presence.

BLACKOUT

TOXIC

~female hospital employee, 30s, on phone to Human Rights
Officer~

Time: The Present

Hello, Mrs. Lammits? This is Rosalie Kovacs calling —
the ICU dietitian from St. James Regional? (pause)

Actually, I was going to say I'm fine, thank you, but
no, I am stressed! And thank you so much for taking my call.
(voice shaky)

Mrs. Lammits, as I mentioned in my email to Human
Rights, I've seen life and death on this job, but this *situation,* in
this environment, in this hospital or *any*, for that matter, has
no place! I find this behaviour extremely inappropriate and
disturbing.

Just to recap: Jane Keepers, our manager, has been
harassing me and some of my colleagues for months now.

Everybody is scared to complain because she holds the power to create work schedules as punishment – schedules that are tough on those who need to get home to families. We've all become 'yes' people to her. And what's more, she is so chummy with the hospital director, Connie Moore, that it's useless to say anything. It's like them against us. This past year I feel I have been hit the worst by her intimidation tactics. Well, up until recently.

Let me explain, Mrs. Lammits, that since last summer I had a pile of doctors' notes for my chest congestion due to blasting frigid air vents, but Jane refused to change my office space as recommended by my physicians. My husband was stressed over this, too. I was coughing a lot, disturbing his sleep, but not only that - we have two young kids. He did not want his wife to get pneumonia. And Jane did not budge on helping us out.

But now, I need to tell you about the new vendor that came to our hospital last week. He was my guest. I had all sorts of hospital approval for Bradley Smith to showcase his product, a breathing device, and I can't even believe this happened, Mrs. Lammits. Jane Keepers approached us during one of Bradley's demonstrations. She stomped forward like a general in high army boots coming at us with one finger raised high on one hand, and with a clenched fist on the other. Then, through a tight jaw she bellowed, 'What's **this** about?'' in the rudest possible way.

Bradley was stunned. He's only twenty-two, Mrs. Lammits, and this is his first 'real' job. He was polite and he knew his product well. Admittedly, he was a nervous, and through my experience with patients, I gathered he fell somewhere on the Asperger's spectrum. I wanted to give him a chance, and encouraged him to relax.

After Jane's bullying performance, Bradley was shaking, and ironically, he couldn't catch his breath. He started to gasp. He looked like he was about to pass out. It appears he had a panic attack, right there! I told him it was okay to stop, and sit down. He lowered his head and I could see sweat marks on the back of his collared shirt.

Mrs. Lammits, Bradley Smith had to go home. When I contacted him, his sister took the call, and said Bradley was unwell. Eventually, he took an entire week off work because he was traumatized by this woman's toxic attitude. It shook his self-esteem, which was fragile to begin with. His sister explained his family had such hopes for him, and they and his therapist were rooting for him in this field of work.

Maybe he's got issues - who doesn't these days? But still, this is a workplace, and not a war zone. Everyone deserves respect, wouldn't you agree? What can I do, Mrs. Lammits and how can I make changes here? The job itself is stressful enough. We don't need additional pressures like being disrespected and harassed. And think of the message that behaviour sends to the sick as well as to healthy people.

Oh, Mrs. Lammits – just hold on a second – there's a text coming across the top of my phone screen; I need to view it, because I noticed Bradley's name pop up.

(with nervous energy)

Bradley Smith has just been admitted to hospital for a suicide attempt! It's his sister letting me know. Oh no! His family was so proud of him venturing on this new job…until that toxic, insensitive woman, Jane Keepers, pushed him over the edge.

Oh, the poor guy, Mrs. Lammits. Please help us…

BLACKOUT

SISTERS

~Woman, 40s, delivers a community speech~

Time: The Present

My name is Sasha. My sister is Ruta. We were born the same year, 1975, but we are not twins. Ruta is the older sister born January 6, and I was born that same calendar year, December 24th. Yes, our mother had quite a year! Happily, she had great support from our dad.

In our teens Ruta and I were teased as the 'calendar girls' yet we lived as far from that meme as one could image. Ruta painted, and I sewed. We were quite good at our passions. Since we required strong light, our parents turned our home conservatory into a workshop for us to polish our talents. We worked side by side, communicated like we *were* twins attached with an invisible umbilical cord, not to our mother, but to each other.

During breaks, we discussed our dreams. Ruta wanted children, someday. I didn't. Admittedly, we found that strange. We imagined, for sure, having children would be something we would agree on. But we didn't.

Ruta moved from our Ontario town of London to New York City to study architecture, and painting remained her passion. She fell for her professor, Bernard Schwartz, and they married. They became partners in a successful architectural firm. And her watercolours, those beautiful, pastel cityscapes, sold in galleries in SoHo, Lower Manhattan. They were considered *avant-garde,* and in demand by visiting Europeans. Life was good.

Since I was not as academically inclined as Ruta, I focused on my sewing until my designs became noticed at the 'One-of-a-Kind' Craft Show in Toronto. I relocated to nearby Hamilton, and found a small space on James Street to continue my craft business. Contractor Joe, hammering next door as part of the area's gentrification project, popped in on his lunch to chat. Who knew how life would turn out? This burly, dark-haired hunk who could make anything out of wood, offered to build me a new sewing table. The two of us teamed up, and moved in together. It was love at first *fight* with us; we disagreed about the idea of raising kids! Born into a large Italian family, Joe was eager to be a dad. Eventually, we compromised with a couple of Shih-Tzu: Marcus and Rudy. Life was good for us, too.

My beloved sister Ruta and I *Skyped* often. Even though we missed each other terribly, we knew we were blessed with this advancing technology, and both of us were living our dreams.

Three years into their marriage, Ruta and Bernie, became parents of twin daughters. Regina was a brunette with pronounced eyebrows, even for a little kid, and Rachel was fair with freckles and strawberry hair. We delighted in the fact the girls, being fraternal, could each express her unique self. Ruta and Bernie hired live-in nanny, Tala. Successful in their creative industry, they designed condos with French flair, and homes with fluted columns to grace various parts of their metropolis.

In the winter of 2013, my sis and her hubby took their darling girls to the theatre for the classic, *Nutcracker,* to enjoy sparkling, tiny ballerinas spin around giant icicles. Afterwards, they had planned to wander the downtown, together, as two lovers would. So, after ice cream for the girls, they put their seven-year-old darlings and Tala into a cab, promising to return within the hour.

It was Christmas Eve, and the city was beautifully lit;

the evening was enchanting, indeed. When I imagine it, I can almost see them now, collars turned up, walking arm in arm, holding each other as they tread through the icy streets. Being specialists in design, Ruta and Bernie would view the surrounding structures with a keen and critical eye, enjoying both the aesthetic appeal and functionality of the buildings.

The call I received on my birthday that year came on my mobile from my parents. Joe and I had just cuddled up to a cozy fire in a ski chalet out of town. The news shocked us beyond anything we could imagine. Ruta and Bernie were gone, dead. Killed on the street in New York city.

Witnesses reported they heard Bernie shout, noticed him look up as shards of glass popped and shattered from a tower to the pavement. Bernie pulled Ruta by the shoulders out of the way. He couldn't save her. And he couldn't save himself, either. Bystanders screamed danger as Bernie backed onto the road and was mowed down by a rushing taxi.

Within a three-minute period, my nieces became orphans. On *this* night before Christmas, did visions of sugar plums dance in *their* heads? I ached at the thought of them having to be told the next morning. For the next year, the girls were placed into several foster homes. And, after much haranguing with immigration lawyers and courts, Joe and I finally became legal guardians. I ended up as the mother I never wanted or expected to be. Just a few years ago, I couldn't have imagined such a thing: I stepped into the role which *elevated* me and the memory of my dear sister, Ruta.

Nanny Tala offered to remain with us, so we moved the three of them to our Hamilton home. Joe worked like crazy after hours that year to get our place ready. The twins delighted in the pups and each took one for her own. We are all healing. The sisters are loved.

But they needed counselling, then, and still do. That's why I'm here with our story at this new Children's Bereavement Centre. Children need on-going support for their profound losses. Thank you for your donations and endorsement of this building, this drop-in *home* of comfort and understanding.

I'll take your questions now...

BLACKOUT

SYLVIA VALEVICIUS

ANXIETY

~male, late 30s, gives a TEDX speech~

Time: The Present

Good Morning! You're all looking at me to solve this problem of ANXIETY. A problem everyone of you in this auditorium has experienced, *guaranteed* - not even once - but plenty of times during your lifetime, and one which I am experiencing right now! (pause for laughter)

But not for long! And I'll explain why, but first let me tell you that I am not a doctor but a clinical psychologist who hears this complaint almost daily.

So, what *exactly* is anxiety, and why is it so powerful? By the way, any of you here today wake up at 3:05 am. on a consistent basis? And I don't mean those who work in early morning television. You know that's a *classic* symptom, don't you? Waking up in the middle of the night, and then struggling to get back to sleep.

Anxiety begins in the mind as a thought. That thought then turns into a feeling. And the feeling turns into a belief. What a jump from reality! By hosting the thought, now a belief, you give it control to master you. Suddenly you're aware of sweat on your brow, and dampness under your armpits. You'd rather have some moisture in your mouth which has dried up like the Sahara Desert. Without its regular saliva, your tongue is heavy.

These physical manifestations occur because of a thought! Wow, did you ever think your thoughts were that powerful? Did you ever give them such credit, before you became a victim of anxiety? Just think about that thought.

Who's the boss, here? Your thoughts, or the power with which you endow them? Well, if thoughts are that powerful, then why not use them in a way that will help you achieve your goals, make you happier, not stress you out?

Alright, there are strategies you can use to rid yourself of unwelcome thoughts, and the resulting anxiety. First, you need to understand that anxiety is an internal build-up, a collection of thought-related feelings which have taken over and rushed down to a sensitive part of your body. No not *that* one --to the gut! Now with all these feelings in your gut shoving each other around causing trouble, of course you need to get rid of them. Well, you can't spray them away like you can mosquitoes, but you can make them disperse, and you must. What is one sure immediate way? I'd like to say, like a teacher might – hands up who knows – but I don't have time to take your answers today so I'll just make that a rhetorical question, and tell you, unless you want to shout it out – I won't mind that. (pause)

So? (pause) Humour, yes, humour. As soon as you laugh, you've just kicked about a thousand lingering anxiety midges in the butt, right out the back door. Feel it now? Gone, relief! Because these nasty little feelings, born from your thoughts, cannot survive in such a *poisonous* environment as **laughter.** Feel your saliva flow back happily into your mouth, and your tongue is liberated, no longer stuck – you are free to speak your mind again – which is your positive mind!

So, strategy number one: don't give thoughts such power, but if you do, make sure you think of something funny, crazy even, right away. And while you're thinking of something funny, you are *actively* pursuing something, not just passively allowing negative thoughts to invade your mind. Thus, the power of *productivity* is at work.

Productivity can take many forms. From funny thoughts, to physical action. Walking, running, even deep breathing, dissipates the build-up of those unwanted trouble-makers in your gut. You sweep away the physical negative feelings, and the mind clears, the anxiety melts.

Look at the anxiety as negative *energy* stored inside you. Energy is great but it needs to be used properly, in a positive, healthy way. It can't just sit in your gut and fester. That is pollution, for sure.

Another strategy to rid yourself of anxiety is to take the focus off you, and place it on another. No worries, I'm not suggesting you give someone else your anxiety; I'm saying your anxiety disappears when you're concerned about another's welfare. Take kids for instance. Many of you have children, I imagine, or work with children, or have grandchildren. I'm a dad of two young boys, myself. And when I am with them at the park, pushing them on a swing, it is therapy for me. I am in the moment.

You can also put yourself into the moment of peace by breathing deeply. I know this is not a newsflash, you've heard it before, but it is a strategy that works. Lie down, if you're alone, or you can do it standing if you're in public, and slowly count in: one, two, three, four; out: five, six, seven, eight. It works! Try it now. Breathe and count. Breathe and count. Breathe and count.

Another piece of magic to rid yourself of anxiety is the word, NO! Practise saying it until it feels natural. When you are burdened by others, halt, and say, NO. You can throw in a 'thanks!'

And, in a worse case scenario, you can see your doctor… who will probably tell you just what I did. Remember to laugh. It's your best weapon against anxiety! Have a great day of freedom!

BLACKOUT

SHE LEFT ME

~male 60s, in hospice with terminal illness, reminisces to nurse~

Time: The Present...recalling the Past

I quit drinking for her. I know you're not supposed to quit drinking for anybody else, but she gave me an ultimatum. That's when I realized I wanted her more than my daily vodka. I wanted her, forever.

She was young, and she was beautiful. I wasn't much for younger women, then; I thought they were, as the saying goes, 'young and foolish.'

I was about forty, a divorce behind me, and over a relationship with an older woman. I was down on my luck as a contractor, a home builder, and through my fortunate connection with the realtor brother of her husband, I got a job in her Victorian house as a renovator. That's when I got to know her. She was around twenty-six, smart, funny, and good-hearted. She invited forlorn me to stay for dinner occasionally – join her and the kids. I was building them a playroom. I took her up on her offer, but had trouble making eye-contact. Also, I wondered if her heart-surgeon husband would show up unannounced, barge in through the back door, and find me sitting at his table.

Her husband hired me, but he was rarely around. Eventually, she and I talked for hours after I knocked off work. We became friends. She was lonely, and pretty much deserted. She didn't know this, but I had the inside information from her brother-in-law that her husband was shacking-up with his office nurse. I tried to shield her from this news.

Her husband was insane to look anywhere else. As a mother, she was tender and loving with the children. And as a woman she was fashionable, sexy, great figure, too. I guess some guys are born to be womanizers. I know I seem to have a checkered past, myself, but I was faithful in my relationships. So, I couldn't help judging him.

When the shit hit the fan and it became clear they were divorcing, her small children went to their father's new place on weekends. That's when she and I would go for drives in the country. She cried and cried. I didn't mind. I felt she was genuine, an old soul, grieving the loss of her marriage and her future, family plans.

Foolishly, we thought she'd have a divorce in a few months. By now, we were emotionally attached. My work at her home completed and so not to spoil her chances for alimony, we agreed I should disappear. I took a two-month road trip, alone, in my van, down to the United States, across to the Pacific coast, and back up to Canada. I taped my experiences, those days on cassettes, and sent her them. In some, I was the one who cried, my voice cracking with loneliness. I ached with missing her. I carried her everywhere on the trip with me even into the jazz bars of New Orleans.

It took four years for her divorce. We had to play the 'cloak and dagger' game. To gain *any* alimony, she wasn't to be seen with another man. The law, back then, was not in a woman's favour, not like it is today. So, after her children were asleep, I came nightly like a ghost to the side door of her house. I parked far away and walked to her home in the dark; I left by two in the morning.

Weekends when the kids were away, we drove up north, every season. I owned a place with a friend: a little fishing cabin in the woods. Of course, we had the space to ourselves. She experienced many 'firsts' with me: summer paddling in a canoe, slurping raw oysters, and winters, a wonderland of snow piled high, with our cozy, franklin stove crackling inside. Our most intimate moments were totally fulfilling for her. I'm not just a dying old guy who's boasting. I was there!

But she wasn't young and foolish, at all. She was young and ambitious. With her kids in school, she began university classes, one at a time. Eventually, she was in school full-time.

Our breakup was long and painful. For both of us. Our timing wasn't right. I know she had to explore what she could achieve. I couldn't hold this against her. Her husband might have been the biggest jerk on the planet, but on the other hand, their breakup gave me the opportunity to know her and to love her.

I often wonder if she regretted leaving me. I could have made her happy, but didn't get the chance, because she left me.

Yet, I just know in my heart she LOVED me…*more* than her husband, and I can live with that thought. (wipes a tear)

BLACKOUT

THE PURSE

~female, 60s, reads her diary piece in a *Happiness Project* Group~

Time: The Present

We were in a real Toronto castle for my son's winter wedding. Snowflakes drifted outside, everyone swirled inside. A few gentlemen even wore top hats and capes, others swinging kilts, but most turned out in the usual tuxedos. Ladies glittered in their evening wear with flirty, short or long flowing hemlines. The jazzy band of joyful brass instruments kept the ballroom swaying. But now we were arranged at the round tables for the dessert and cake-cutting.

Seated on my right, my mother, always with an eye for beauty, nudges me: "Who's that pretty girl in the red gown beside you?" she loudly whispers. Just like that, out of the blue. On my left, unaware of mother's question my daughter flirts with her suave husband. I tell mother it's her granddaughter, Caroline, and she glares at me askance, as if I'm lying. Then she traces her fork around her plate.

Disconcerted, mother lifts her shoulder, shifts direction; her eyes search the darker side of the room, distant tables, for someone she expects to find. She now forgets I am beside her. She is alone, blank, while glasses clink as someone calls for attention.

Earlier that day in our downtown Marriott hotel room mother rushes to change out of her morning clothes. I reach forward to help, but she swipes at me, "I can do this myself," she insists. I am sad and embarrassed to see her lacy bra shoved high on her chest not covering what it should.

She's in a hurry to head down the corridor to the suite of the father-of-the-groom where my ex-husband and his third wife hold court. Later when I tap on their door to collect her, mother is childlike happy. She laughs, waves me in with her lighted cigarette held high. The film of smoke alarms me. I cough to make a point. The three of them pull a face as I gather mother's wrap, her beaded purse, and firmly escort her from this private soiree to the reception. Mother calls me a party-pooper. Of course, she forgets the touchy past, the long-ago trauma of my being *first* wife. It's on these occasions humour and civility become internal beasts of burden. Decorum reigns.

Some weeks later, mother phones me to report the

man who stares at her from her kitchen's television screen. She's annoyed he's able to watch her without her permission. I reassure her. It's only one-way, I say. Are you sure, are you sure, she continues to grill me. Yes, Mom. *You're* staring at him. Turn it off, I tell her.

Her phone calls to me increase in intensity. One Saturday night we begin a new argument. She prepares to go to the Mall. Oh, what should I wear, she wonders aloud. I tell her everything is closed, it's midnight. She scoffs. She doesn't believe me. I tell her to open her bedroom drapes. "What do you see?" I ask.

"It's dark, today," she replies. "Probably raining out there." I tell her it's the middle of the night, to put on her nightie, and go to bed. She's a rebel, my mother.

I begin to consider mother should no longer be driving. This topic creates fireworks. Mother is outraged. For the time being my brothers and I let it go. *Is it worth the fight?*

In June I drive several hours to the dance recital of my young granddaughters, and stay until the next day. When I return home, a niece calls to inform me mother is hospitalized. She had tripped in her garden the Friday evening, and spent the night outside on the ground discovered only in the morning by a townhouse neighbour.

My heart breaks. I rush to her side as she is in recovery from surgery for a broken femur. My older brother, her *power of attorney*, has retreated to his cottage leaving a signed DNR form at the nurses' station. Given that brother and I are not on speaking terms, I am confused by these orders, and hurt, as well. It seems he expected her to die during the operation. *To die, from a broken leg?*

High on morphine mother regains some consciousness, and turns to notice me. It's her eighty-sixth birthday; I hold up her gift to show her a straw, cowgirl hat in her favourite turquoise. Then I hold her hand. I also wonder why no other family member is present. Just me and mother. As her only daughter it's for these moments I'd always yearned, albeit, not under such dire circumstances.

She compliments me, says I am beautiful. I look at her, stretched out post-op, blue *OR* cap partially covering her golden hair. Her blue eyes, now stoned, are still compelling in their intense paleness. She claims to love me. This revelation she slurs in English, not in her Baltic tongue. Never comfortable expressing verbal love, mother delivers this sentiment in the adopted language which must feel okay to her. As I stand beside her gurney, her words fill me with a wicked gratitude for the drug's ardent effect.

She survives the procedure and is moved to the floor as a regular patient. But there is nothing regular about my mother. She doesn't eat. She falls out of bed, and hospital staff put restraints on her wrists. They put invisible ones around my throat. I have difficulty swallowing as I come to spoon-feed my mother. She only eats for you the staff tell me. My guilt swells as I come from a neighbouring town, not as available as I would like. My eldest brother is intubated in a Toronto rehabilitation facility which I visit several days a week. I commute between cities where loved-ones suffer.

Relatives begin to visit mother. A respite for me. My brother's wife brings delicious home-prepared meals. Still, mother spits them out. I offer excuses to my sister-in-law: not much appetite when one's in pain; so grateful for this extra help.

After a few days' absence, with dry-mouthed anxiety, I return to the hospital. I see both sides of the hallway lined with wheelchairs and poles. Why aren't patients in their rooms? Offensive odours waft around me. The hallway smells like shit, literally. I look right and left, and gaze upon the back of a head which appears a familiar shape… I shudder. *No, it can't be… not my mother.* Greasy, grey hair, pasted flat at the crown. Deep in my gut I think it *is* her, but never in her life had she looked that way, neglected, dishevelled, not my silver and gold vivacious mother. A nurse approaches and I hide my panic, explain I am looking for Mrs. R.

"Why, she's right here!" The nurse offers perfunctory cheer which exacerbates my shock. "Let's wheel her into her room, shall we?"

I nod, relieved.

Now that I walk alongside the wheelchair, I see her face, clearly. Now there is no doubt this frail, shabby person in a blue hospital gown is, indeed, my mother. I am light-headed, barely manage to contain myself, or the waves of nausea rising in my windpipe.

"Let's not forget her purse," says this animated attendant.

I look around, my head bobbing up and down in agreement, eager to believe the staff pays attention to my mother's belongings. Yet I see nothing in the surroundings which resembles mother's tan, leather purse.

"I don't see it anywhere," I say, flustered.

With a self-satisfied grin, the nurse dramatically hoists a rubber bag of urine off the floor, and hooks it onto the pole attached to the wheelchair.

"Here we are," she says, singsong style, and pushes mom forward towards a room. I stand there observing *such efficiency* in action. I am stunned, speechless and sad.

Finally, we settle in mom's room, I on the edge of her bed, and she still in the chair. The sun streams through the large hospital window and spreads a welcome light on mother's tiny face. She appears luminous, weightless. I look her in the eye and ask if she knows my name. Mother smiles sweetly, then chuckles and waves it off - my foolish question. I see in her face she is stuck for an answer. For years afterwards, I am ashamed of this moment. Ashamed of putting my mother on the spot. My memory punishes me for insensitivity of her undiagnosed, but evident dementia.

"Get me out of here!" mother begs. I explain only her son can do that, not me, I am not in charge. *I am merely the daughter, the one with no power.* Naturally, she doesn't get it. Poor mom pleads she must get home to her husband, to Walter, so they can finish their work in the garden, together. He is waiting for her, she tells me. He is waiting...

I don't tell her my father is not at home. I don't remind her he has been lying in the cemetery for ten years. But I think to myself perhaps now he waits there for her to join him. And, perhaps now she knows this.

That day in hospital was the last time I saw my mother alive.

THE END

Post Script:

My parents lie together. A small, round portrait of their young, wedding-day smiling faces, which began their fifty-seven-year union, is mounted on their tombstone. Mother's dress and brimmed hat are pale blue which match her eyes. Out of frame, I know she holds my beaming father's hand, and her blue, cloth purse rests in her lap.

BLACKOUT

AND THEN I FELL

~A 60-ish bubbly woman shares an
experience with her knitting-group members~

Time: The Present

According to my grown-up son Chuck, the good part of being a hockey grandma is that it keeps me *active*. And with this philosophy in mind, Chuck puts me to good use!

Last summer, Chuck enrolled my eight-year-old grandson into a hockey, power-skate program. Billy had shown such promise during the winter season, Chuck, who's both the team's coach, as well as Billy's dad, wanted him to keep those skills sharp. Since the parents worked at full-time careers, this *exciting opportunity* fell to me: pick him up from summer camp, collect his mammoth hockey bag from his house, grab the hockey stick, the water bottle, and drive him half-way across the city to the ice arena.

Being the obliging mom and grandma that I am, I agreed to help. Yet, I had concerns. When it came time to dress this little star, I'd never figure out how to manage the pads, pants, and other uniform parts which fell to me to layer on my sweet grandkid. I was clueless. Fortunately, Chuck emailed me instructions, although he neglected to mention I'd need a small pair of scissors to snip the tape which winds around the knee socks. Hand-ripping was too tough, so I used my teeth, instead. Oh yeah, I sure did worry I might uncap my new dental crown! But, acting like a hero grandma, I even laced Billy's skates myself, balancing each bladed-foot between my knees and pulled tight. Everything went swimmingly...well... all set for smooth skating.

Just one last thing. I didn't have the strength in my thumbs to fasten the snaps on that glossy, rock-hard helmet. Who knew a woman had to have *thumbs* in good shape, too? What to do?

I turned to a hockey dad in the dressing room, a radio broadcaster with a flexible daytime schedule. He was there with his son who was one of Billy's winter teammates, so I knew the dad, slightly. It fell to me to straddle the two positions: the 'I got this' kick-ass woman, and the 'damsel in distress' to appeal to his male ego. I chose the latter and asked for help. He obliged with a sexy smile, and turned into *Ryan Reynolds* before my eyes.

When the boys played, we watched their game from the side-lines. This lovely *Ryan* simply delighted me - a most welcome distraction. While standing beside him I hardly even noticed the usual cold of the ice-rink aching through my joints. In fact, his heart-melting smile left me, rather shamelessly, weak in the knees.

And then I fell. Heart first, into a crazy teenage crush on this forty-something dad. The age of my son! He was the total package: friendly, attentive, with a cute kid, and nary a wife in sight. It was easy to fall into a fantasy.

Let me make one thing crystal clear: I don't chase after married men, but being single, occasionally those fantasies chase me. Suddenly, I revelled in being attractive, interesting, and young! I displayed my dazzling personality to this dad, and felt his interest, in return.

After the practice, as we were leaving the arena, the boys ran ahead. A new group of skaters were coming in, pulling their bulky equipment bags. I walked along the narrow hallway with this dimple-cheeked dad, both of us keeping a brisk pace, side by side, towards the front of the building. Upbeat, laughing!

AND THEN I FELL.

Like a jump horse collapsing under a missed hurdle, I crashed to my knees onto the concrete walkway. In a flash, I had broken my stride, tripped, and flipped over a humungous hockey bag. A boy in front of me who had turned to enter a dressing room suddenly stopped. Since I had been trotting straight ahead, there was no place to get out of his way. I was down.

The charming dad, his *Ryan* smile still frozen on his face, looked down, and waited for me to pop up like a Walmart *Bop Bag* or the youthful woman I was impersonating. He didn't realize I transformed into a deflated senior, and lacked the knee-strength to gather myself from the ground.

Shamed like a naughty puppy, I barely looked at him, but asked: "Could you help me up, please?" Of course, he was chivalrous.

I snapped into a cold, body *reality* check. I blew out a knee, and damaged my pride with my inflated fantasies of youth.

Now, the newsflash is: can't keep a good woman down. This grandma's back again being *active*. And things are heating up once again. But that's another story...

BLACKOUT

ABOUT THE AUTHOR

Sylvia Valevicius is a graduate of McMaster University, B.A., MA., and the University of Toronto, B.Ed. She enjoys books, art, music, language study, fitness, fresh air walks by the lake, and loves her family most of all. To learn more about her life and varied careers, Sylvia invites you to read her autobiography, a bit of a literary door-stopper, but packed with photos and ideas!

Memoir of Hope & Resilience: Passionate Late-Bloomer Talks Life, Literature, and Personal Empowerment. (pub. 2016, Verdant Isle Production)– available from your Amazon, (welcome to read the reviews) or from Sylvia's website for US readers – both print & digital. Also, available from Oakville Public Library, Oakville, ON. Canada.

Sylvia also published *Monologues for Youth*, Volumes 1 & 2, (2014, 2015) available on Amazon.

Website: whoissylvia.net (email: sylvia@whoissylvia.net)

Twitter: @Jtosnest

Instagram: @sylviamvalevicius

Goodreads (author & reviewer) and Amazon Author.

Occasional actor known as: Joey T. Oliver (to audition, think Helen Mirren roles: mature, sexy & humorous)

Sylvia is currently writing a novel set in the lovely town where she lives, Oakville, Ontario. The 'working' title: *The World of SIN* ☺

*Kindly remember to leave a review, or your opinion, of this book (or any others mentioned here) on any Amazon site, or Goodreads site, your blog, the library page, etc. Great wishes to you for the best Karma from a grateful author!